WINDOW OF BABEL

BORCHE PANOV

Červená Barva Press
Somerville, Massachusetts

Copyright © 2024 by Borche Panov

All rights reserved. No part of this book may be reproduced in any manner without written consent except for the quotation of short passages used inside of an article, criticism, or review.

Červená Barva Press
P.O. Box 440357
W. Somerville, MA 02144

www.cervenabarvapress.com

Bookstore: www.thelostbookshelf.com

Production: Allison O'Keefe

Cover Art: "Tower of Babel" by Witold Zakrzewski

ISBN: 978-1-950063-83-3

Library of Congress Control Number: 2024932195

Selection of poems by
Daniela Andonovska-Trajkovska

Translated from Macedonian
into English language by
Daniela Andonovska-Trajkovska

CONTENTS

GOD LIKE AN ABSTRACT NOUN

God Like an Abstract Noun	3
She-Wolf	4
Universal Language	5
Crucifixion of Time	6
Russian Roulette	7
Milk of Mercy*	8
My Mother	9

THE WINDOW OF BABEL

The Window of Babel	13
The Sceleton of the Future	14
Apocalypse	16
The Soft Hydrogen of the Words	17
Hydrogen	18
A Poem About the Sheep That Grazes Green Grass From Our Hands	19
A Room of My Time Zones	21
The Angel of Breathing	23
Sun	24
A Pitcher	25
Blood That Juggles With 8000 Poetic Thoughts	26
In Praise of Folly and the Hormons Ghrelin and Leptin	28

THE ANT AND SISYPHUS

The Ant and Sisyphus	33
Solid Construction	34
Mirrors, Mental Hygiene	35
Today, a Man Should Remember	38
I Was Dreaming About My Mammoth Tusks	39
Lethargy	41
Runner	42

MÖBIUS STRIP

Eternal Rain	45
With the Whole Time I Speak to You	47
Möbius Strip	48
When the Clock Hands Overlap	49
Chain of Sand	50
Little Vigil Lamp	51
Red and White Blood Cells	52

GEOMETRICAL CAT

Shadow Play	55
Geometrical Cat	56
The Bald Town	57
The Queen of the Transparent Chess Pieces	59
What Did Charlie Ch. See From the Upside Down	60
Black-and-White Rushing Town	62
A Room Envelope	63
Symmetrical Double	64

HORIZON OF LIVING

Horizon of Living	67
Other-Sided Horse	68
Beat	69
Fog 1	70
Fog 2	70
Little Collar Dove	71
Double	72

MICHELANGELO AND MY FATHER'S HEART

Michelangelo and My Father's Heart	75
Glimpse	76
Birthday Greeting	77

The Night Face of the Sun	78
Simultaneous Time	79
Eight Minutes of Day in the Night	80
The White Mouse of the Truth	81

SCULPTURE OF BREATHING

Verb (^{In})Tense(^{Ness})	85
Threshing Time	86
Cat Times	87
Sculpture Of Breathing	89
Fossil Hesitation	90
The Poet's Angel	91
Ars Poetica	92
Poetry	93
Origami	94
Diptych of the Sorrow	95
House Spider Web	96
Reading From Right to Left	97

BENEVOLENCE HANGER

Benevolence Hanger	101
Listen Rooster*	102
The Artist Of Death	104
The Morning Line	106
Bread	107
Everlasting Moment	108
Gilgamesh	109

ABOUT THE AUTHOR
ABOUT THE TRANSLATOR

WINDOW OF BABEL

GOD LIKE AN ABSTRACT NOUN

GOD LIKE AN ABSTRACT NOUN

clay and water dry fast
and time would pass through you brutally
only a breath can hold it and turn it into you

time is time only if it is a personal noun

God is an abstract noun
clay and water are concrete nouns
the breath is abstract too
it is concrete only if it gets misty on the mirror
to indicate that you are alive
and if you are not, then it is more abstract than the
death itself
concrete nouns cannot even die without the
abstract ones
nor can think or feel without them
nor will know what day it is on the calendar
or in what season
the lexis of the bitter fruits blooms and becomes
ripe

clay and water will dry fast in the language
in which God
would be an abstract noun

SHE-WOLF

1.

poetry is just like my little dog
when she is happy she rears up on her hind legs
and she is howling with a hoarse voice to make me
remember
that she used to be a she-wolf
and I used to be a cave man

2.

poetry has a growling stomach
but she never shows that she is famished
the most important thing for her is
to jump on the empty chair
and to be a part of the family around the dining
table

UNIVERSAL LANGUAGE

every day
I stumble over the pebble
that I keep under my tongue
a little pebble like the apple seed
I inherited
from the expulsion from Eden

we left the paradise
with the language of the serpents

CRUCIFIXION OF TIME

if we crucify the word
will it become a body again
to make us feel all the joy
with which God was creating the world
and all the pain
with which he sacrificed his own son

if we crucify the time
will there be someone who will resurrect
to be a space for a whole civilization

RUSSIAN ROULETTE

many years ago
I have sent myself a letter
a letter addressed to me
in this foggy morning
unexpectedly
I thought about that letter
but I couldn't remember what was written inside
we can proceed
with the Russian roulette
there is a third player between us now
the third player that was missing

MILK OF MERCY*

A ragged and toothless old man
and a young woman, like two rings
of a chain, grey for centuries,
hovering
in an embrace of a breastfeeding woman and a martyr
thirsty sucking from a breast full of milk –
two rings, like two destinies – convicted twice,
but why amidst loud thoughts
in concentric circles they are swirling again,
I hear an echo saying what a pitiable image
of a shameless old man and an easy woman
that entices and lures in a bizarre manner this is,
and I wonder why nobody
perceives it as an act of merciful love
in which a young mother – a daughter or a granddaughter,
with warm milk refused by a nursling,
is fiercely struggling to keep a prisoner alive,
sentenced to thirst and hunger
in a prison cell, in darkness, in a gulag,
a bastille or Treblinka of death
and why in the middle of that swirl that is contracting
and sifting life and plucking everything,
rarely would someone think that the painter
the gentlest story in front of our eyes –
behind our licentious pupils has painted for us
like lips that are sucking thirsty the milk of mercy
that each of us has innocently tasted at least once
in a lifetime

*inspired by a painting from unknown artist

MY MOTHER

I asked my mother on the phone
how she was
she was preparing for the death she said
whose death – I asked her again
Mine – she said
I was struck dumb
and told her not to speak to me like that
it doesn't mean she was dead she said
if she went to the store
to buy a nice white sheet
and then I thought about my art teacher
who was telling us that white color
motherly hugs all the colors
for a new beginning of the end of what we don't
know
it was my teacher who always asked us
if we had seen the white bird
that had been detaching from the canvas
to inhabit a warm meridian in one of us

in the middle of the branches of the vocal cords
that bird of paradise will sing for you one day
and you will see Adam biting the apple

paint that apple with a feeling
that the bite of immortality is stuck in your throat
while you are becoming aware of your mortality

the teacher was talking to me and I was
listening to my mother
making jokes about her death
from the warm meridian of my childhood

THE WINDOW OF BABEL

THE WINDOW OF BABEL

Above a little and forgotten room – on the bottom of the Earth,
the sky is like the Tower of Babel
cities - placed on the top of each other and linked in non-reaching rings
rising endlessly. The heights on the top
speak one language only. In that little room, oh dear God,
I convinced myself that You are that language
with the words that we dream in, sometimes,
and we wake up more or less occasionally. I wondered,
when did clay start to grow in my mouth,
and moss on my tongue as well and when will the
past and the future stop hurting me
like the ball-and-socket joint that rubs itself without
the cartilage of the presence?
And I wondered, could you, oh dear God,
dream in my words,
and could I wake up myself into yours at least once?
Suddenly, a bird hit the glass.
The sky is here, as well, I encouraged myself, and I opened the window...

THE SCELETON OF THE FUTURE

the space elongates through the windows
the sky plumb bob falls and breaks the three dots
at the end of the sentence of the horizon
the chisel falls from my hands too
the chisel with which I chip the stones of the dream

a man should stop for a moment
to see the creations of his breath

with curtains blown like white sails
my rooms sail on the blue line of the morning
behind the three dots of the time and the space
people sleep waiting for the eternity

the wind is winded up like a spring
in the mechanical toy of the apocalypse
the owl of the prehistory lands at the book shelves
and the tyrannosauruses and the reptiles
still hunt the daylight from our eyes

in the deepest night of our fear
the prayer is like a trap of eyelashes
in which we hold the Sun just for a moment
while a bridge like a dear
jumps from our side
over the fog from which all the war moles
come out one by one
and the sleepwalkers return to us
like a boomerang of the dream

down the sky the theatre of our faces hovers
the walls of the lashes separate us from a world in
which memories are clepsydra of the delusions
that we die being immortal
with all the scenes of catharsis
in which we don't recognize the hell we have
created
while the mechanical key of the wind unscrews
itself

the labyrinth of the deceit is a house of a snail
in his spiral we return to the beginning of Creation
and we wonder
why we are striving to be winners
to snatch everything before others
while from lips to lips the words travel
with all sky lines of the arrivals and the departures
while our shadows congeal on the skeleton of the
future
and we believe we have created time

APOCALYPSE

Are we waiting for the hidden clocks to come,
do we imagine the keys
with which we will go out of the time

Is it enough to sense our pulse with our forefinger
Is the night becoming a dark body of our heart
Is our sleeplessness brightened by the dawn
Are the thoughts chirping to us with the birds
arrayed like notes in the architecture of the forest

What is the proportion of the force
with which our pressure is pushing against the
blood vessels' walls,
if from outside, from the edge of the universe and
the Earth,
on only one square centimeter,
one kilogram of air pressures us every moment

Will the rooms run away from our houses
and in the streets - the cities all in panic,
will the air of this time
and the rivers and the bad odor of the corps in the
dry riverbeds
escape from us

Is God going to be dark at the end of the sky
as a star amoeba collecting our minds
millions of years since the beginning of the dreams

Will we dress up with the peeled Sun
with the Morse code letters of the roller blinds,
and with the last prayer like a skin of a snake
from which the reptile of the apocalypse was born

Is the night becoming a dark body of our heart,
Is our sleeplessness brightened by the dawn,
Are the thoughts chirping to us with the birds
arrayed like notes in the architecture of the forest

THE SOFT HYDROGEN OF THE WORDS

No one knows
when the silence condenses its annual ring
in the wood of my prayer

no one knows
that when I drink joy
I run and I run,
and the sorrow follows me slowly
and it overtakes me - drunk of love

no one knows
that I constantly imagine a wind
and I let the idea
blow through the dreams' hands

no one knows
that one "I" is begging me persistently
to let go the lake of desires,
and I ask him how will we survive the silence
without which the water will not be burning
anymore,
if we know that the hydrogen gets softer,
and the oxygen
raises the flame of our lives
lit by the atoms of the dreams...

HYDROGEN

Hydrogen is the lightest element in nature.
When it burns water is created.
We were born out of that fire, too.

Hydrogen is the lightest element in nature.
God has created the prime burning, as well.
He ignited the prime fire among the words.

Hydrogen is the lightest element in nature.
We have created the heaviest hydrogen:
Protium and Tritium. We have made
the hydrogen bombs out of them.

Hydrogen is the lightest element in nature.
When it burns water is created.
We were born out of that fire, too.

Oh, dear God, let us burn with your fire,
don't let us burn with our fire.

A POEM ABOUT THE SHEEP THAT GRAZES GREEN GRASS FROM OUR HANDS

The light is a cube of shadow in the room
and a cube in the palm
and there is another cube in it
and so on... with no end in sight –
I hold the light which is a cube
and the shadow without which the cube wouldn't
have been a room
But it could also be
a picture of a tree and a window with night
and wind in the leaves and a black night with a
moon
and a sunny day around them
and a window on the blue sky
and a tree in a black night and a moon on the
outside
and so on... with no end in sight
Well it could be the Eiffel Tower over the fog
and transparent bridges from one bank to another
and a city between two weavers and clouds of wool
and sheep that we count on the woollen thread of
the insomnia
like black silhouettes that go through the white
moon
and an angel engraved from distant lights
and wings of an angel - spread on a black-and-
white keyboard
and tones touching us
in silence, or disarray just to make us look at the
sky
and two glass skyscrapers with violet skeletons
that are melting among the screams coming from
the flames
and a black smoke
in the middle of the concentric circles of white
human ashes
and letters with the home address of the death
and invisible planes
and laser sights in the middle of strange

conspiracies
and an ocean wave with vertebras of towns and
little villages on the top
and radioactive migration of the time
and tornados with a hell of silence inside
and gigantic whirls of fear outside
and desolated people
nevertheless
the light is not a shadow of cube in the room
only because of the feeling that we are at home –
there is a moment
that stops with the silence
while everything else is in a rush
through the endless array of the shadows
and so
from the palm – a cube
from the cube – another cube as far as the eyes
can see –
to the two grandmothers of my childhood and the
white woollen God
that they spin like Vivaldi with his four seasons
on the white spindle of the human scream and the
silence –
to the fog in the fleece of a domesticated sheep
that grazes green grass from our palms...

A ROOM OF MY TIME ZONES

my room is stamping stamping
making push-ups
panting panting
because she can't sleep
because she has changed many time zones
far away from home,
she is stamping stamping – compressing soil under
the foundations
to build herself a house
to escape from the windows
to run with the trees and the rain
to go to the circus, to go hand in hand with George,
the dwarf
to spin and to trek the grey merry-go-round of the
world
to catch the flying trapeze
to make salto mortale
and to survive from its own fear
that she will miss the airplane of his dream
that another cataclysm will not happen again
or that she could be recruited in a senseless war
or that someone we love will die
she is stamping stamping
and compressing the prayer
in the foundation of the conviction
that everything will be as it should be
that we will breathe clean air
that there will not be a politician
who will ruin her dreams
that she will not be paralyzed after taking a vaccine
my room is panting panting
making push-ups
to bear all the nightmares of the street
the street with a bulging vein cracked by heroin
and with the eye apples that kill high school
children
with such an ease like in a computer game
or a cartoon with the Road Runner – that mad
street

my room is stamping stamping
panting panting because she can't sleep
she hopes she hopes
that she will not die in a retirement home
inhabited with cockroaches that even in daytime
bustle the gloom of the night

my room is running running
from one time zone to another
at a place in which the evil that had happened,
had not happened yet

my room is panting panting
compressing all the good time
in the foundations of the world of tomorrow
and she prays for the moment
that had already happened somewhere never to
happen again

THE ANGEL OF BREATHING

Sometimes, we are walking on the edge of our lives
like sleepwalkers through some other people's lives
and again, hand by hand with the breath and the sigh
we are holding each other,
just like two worlds that are holding each other
with the breathing
and like white summer clouds
we are interfering with each other –
the one can never see the other
and like the Sun grows on the Moon
through a hopeful high tide in the whisper
and a sad low tide - from the unspoken words,
you tell me that people of today have been lost
and they are leaving their days in the night's mail boxes
like unread letters,
and you tell me that after the long wandering
the embrace is the only mould of the consolation,
you are whispering to me while the eyes
thirsty for their own tears
are binding my soul to the desert of the paper
with the words that are moving like dunes
through the various forms of an ancient wind
indicating that the time comes
the time in which
on the morning threshold of the expectation
I will find the fossil of the day
that remains in two worlds at the same time
worlds that are holding each other hand by hand
all the time
with the breathing only...

SUN

Sun oh Sun
in countless knots you entangle in my head

and in the gloom
when I pull out the longest thread of the sorrow
you are the one that I untangle, again

Sun oh Sun
Will there be enough stitches of days and nights
for us to prevent the unknitting of the writing
to the end of the row
the writing
in which we have embodied ourselves

How many stitches will you unravel
from my shadow to turn me into a ray
like the one with which I have come to the world

Sun oh Sun
blow my ashes in the infinity at the end
and keep blazing
with pure and invisible flame of my soul

be a light that cannot be seen
without which we would have been blind
and interweave yourself
with the knots of my words, too

Sun oh Sun

A PITCHER

A beautiful word is like an earthenware pitcher
Everyone who passes by
Kisses it

And only you
Have left
A lipstick mark on it

BLOOD THAT JUGGLES WITH 8000 POETIC THOUGHTS

a word as a sleepwalker
is walking to the end of the sentence in my dream
and I cannot decide what should I be concerned about more –
about the senselessness
or about the incomprehensible coincidence
with which the sleepwalkers avoid the accident
at the exact moment when it is about to happen

and yet, it's not harmless at all
especially when all takes place
on an overtightened nerve,
and when I have to judge
the safety margin of passing the fierce blood
because I never know
what can possibly disturb my balance
because the night is the traffic rush hour of thoughts

in such a moment, the circus comes to my mind,
when in the summer, in the childhood of my town,
it was coming
and from the car's megaphone was announcing
"A snake 8000 meters long and 80 kilograms heavy,
will be answering your questions, tonight",
because I knew that 8000 thoughts are running through
a human's head per a day,
but no one knows how many thoughts there are per a dream,
when a sleepwalker takes you to the end of the sentence
where you could never be sure that your 80 kilograms
will not kill you when you will not be able to tell yourself
where you are going to wake up, when all of your thoughts
will eventually pass to the other side of the nerve thread

no, no you can't be certain what you should be
concerned about more –
about the senselessness
or about the absurd with which accidently or not,
the accident happens at the exact moment
that holds all dilemmas with which only one of your
words is sleepwalking to the end of an incomprehensible
sentence,
and your blood goes with the circus caravan
on a long exotic travel with even more exotic name
"Blood that Juggles with 8000 Poetic Thoughts"

IN PRAISE OF FOLLY AND THE HORMONS GHRELIN AND LEPTIN

I hold the sky with a string like a helium balloon
"In Praise of Folly" it says
I breathe under a hazmat suit in the middle of viruses
and Folly holds a needle
while holding a speech
in front of the sugar wool in my other hand
with a pink worm, because the wool is pink too
in front of the seconds with white gloves
that drive yellow scooters escaped from a madhouse
in front of the swallow of the future green places
charged like the bullet of the migration is charged with gun powder
and immigration of the people
in front of the shadows of the night that stumble
on the syntax of the meridians
in order to move the time
in front of Ghrelin – the hormone of hunger
inflating the stomachs of the skeleton children
and Leptin - the hormone of inappetence
eating the sugar in the blood of the hungry people

My Folly is holding a speech on the top of the needle
over which the blindfolded angels are dancing
and I argue with the four riders of the apocalypse
whether she should name them
after the hormones of appetite and of inappetence
and whether the white rider
will sow grains on the top of the needle too

My Folly is holding a speech
in front of the storm that twitches its muscles
between the eyebrows
and floods our day with a vague existence
in a reality in which our two hands
are sweeping the street with the beards of the Gods

that have fulfilled our gaps
in a shadow play in the city
crushed from the hands that fall from the sky like
bombs

My Folly is holding a speech in front of the street
sweepers
that polish the marble in which exorcists have their
reflections
politicians, pilots,
psychiatrists, water polo players,
informers, statists and ecologists,
lawyers, prosecutors, court dresses dressed up in
judges
and artists who walk their own theatre like a little
dog
that with its pink little anus under the upright tail
speaks the truth
that the future will return to us from the future soon
like supersonic airplane
that will suddenly stop in the middle of the sky
dropping colored clowns
and the sky will be clear like a tear shed from joy
and that upright tail will be wagging
and that shameless little anus will be talking
insolently
in front of their clients, hamburger statists and
ecologists
that enter with high speed in a train that is faster
than the sound
with a commercial that ruffles like a pierced air wall
and says to us
hush, be quiet, please

My Folly is talking
to a chimney sweeper for whom we cannot say
whether he or his shadow blinks with the eyes of a
beautiful day
to a giraffe that says *Don't walk on the grass*

to the neighbor that hangs the rain along the cloth lines
in order to dry the level of the mad North Sea
and in the middle of Dam in Rotterdam of Erasmus
it says to him *let's clap our hands again, to live to the fullest
and to drink and to eat from the tree of the good and the evil
that serves as a gigantic ecological commercial
like an air wall in the middle of the sky*
and says to us
hushhhh

THE ANT AND SISYPHUS

THE ANT AND SISYPHUS

The ant
was rolling the water drop up the hill
and I, like Sisyphus,
was going down
not knowing whether I would find
the same rock again
with which I had conquered the top

The ant wasn't thinking at all
whether the drop
was hard enough
to be a part of the nonsense

SOLID CONSTRUCTION

incessantly
the dream
winds up
the
key
on
my
back
incessantly
I hit
myself
in walls
and at the end
I come out
of the eyelashes
in
a town
in which
the only
solid construction
is this
dream
in a cadence
of a hush
and a war

MIRRORS, MENTAL HYGIENE

all of a sudden
a gym
settled in my head
- One – Two, Up – Down, Left – Right...
she commands
while I am exercising
- Tell yourself
I am not an automat
but a living human,
she shouts at me
everyday
I shout at the mirror
while that poor thing
supports me
deafly

one – two!
I approach to you
like a mental hygiene
oh you have soap in your eyes

up – down!
how could you be clean
when you look at me
with unclean conscience

left – right!
why should I remember you
when you exist only now
the mirror said to me harshly

one – two!
you are not humming in the morning
and you are not paying attention to me anymore
why
asked me the mirror

up – down!
yes
you can break me
but
it is a firm evidence
that
you are broken inside

left – right!
the mirror
is chewing on its last nerve
and keeps quiet
with a nightmare on its lips
his only consolation
is
that I am aware of that too

one – two!
the mirror
presses my eyes
and in the darkness says to me clearly
- You will never guess who it is!

up – down
since the mirror
has started to shave by heart
I look like a self-slaughter more and more
my friends say
equaltothemirrorequaltothemirrorequaltothemirrorequaltothemirror
equaltothemirror

it has been a while
since my head
was getting full
with emptiness
one day
the mirror told me

- Now, you are equal to me,
from now on you will be happy

left – right!
the mirror is getting bald
more and more each day
and as a revenge
it gives me sharp and thick beard

deafborndeafborndeafborndeafborndeafborn

the mirror was born deaf
but
that is why it has
many healthy subjects

it's good it's good it's good it's good
it's good it's good it's good
it's good

it's good
I said to the mirror
all I had was good
and you didn't even look at me
- Weren't you sleeping?
asked the worm in me...

TODAY, A MAN SHOULD REMEMBER

Today, a man should remember
to turn off the mobile phone, the computer and the internet,
the television, the wars, the murders, the tsunami,
the nuclear power plants that are leaking radioactivity,
the giant mutations of the mollusks
tossed on the shore by a brand-new evolution,
the little and the big dictators
that juggle with the fossils of the history
like with decapitated human heads
that stare into our eyes shamelessly
and tell us jokes about Houdini,
and then - the polar vortex
that stops the play of the lake waves,
and carves the iconostasis of the frozen Dante's hell, and then - the ozone holes and the light that turns us into ashes
like a film tape with the Sun that we have given up long time ago,
and then - the digital alarm clock as well,
the shaving machine and the alarms –
simply – all the electronics around us,
in which we dive deep into like electrons in binary sequences
that narrate us on the monitors like inconsistent many samples of "I",
except –
If he could remember to replace the pacemakers' battery
on time,
if his heart is weak.
Then, he could forget the time
and make his first footprints on the innocence of the snow...

I WAS DREAMING ABOUT MY MAMMOTH TUSKS

I am dreaming about my mammoth tusks.

The zoologist from the future
was reading the season changes on my tusks –
the bright short summers and the dark winters.

The right tusk of my dream
was shorter, because I was right-handed,
with my right tusk I was stripping the bark of the
trees, and I was cutting the trees,
and I was opening the road of time
and I was digging my grave.

I used to be big like God, but I didn't hunt anything,
Nevertheless, the time came when I was hunted
because of my teeth.

They turned my teeth into totems and idols,
little spoons and forks of ivory
engraved with the soft faces of their queens,
little combs and hair needles, erotic scenes carved
on the
little jewelry boxes in which the women got
undressed,
because a woman is naked only when she takes off
her jewelry,
the covers and the handles of the sharp knives and
swords,
Biblical gospels on the covers of the holy books,
Jesus was crucified on my tusk, too,
they made saints, and papal thrones
and holy Buddhas, all from ivory, even the chess
pieces among which they were hunting their
enemies were made of my tusks.

I am one of the extinct species.
When in the morning, I cannot decide
whether to wake up as a poet for one more day,
I am weighted down by my tusks – each of my
tusks is 100 kilograms of sleeplessness
as heavy as the crystallized tissue of my memories.

LETHARGY

like a sweeper
that sweeps
the bad dreams
of the night
the town awakens me
on the park bench
and says
Move, you wanderer,
make a space
for this old man
and we were sitting
with our thoughts
like with empty streets
between us
with childish carelessness
the dawn was sitting as well
but for a while
because this bench
became too small
when the day
sat beside us
like an asthmatic
whose breath
is shortened
by everyone
and here it is
a thought
like a dog on a leash
is dragging
my lethargic body
from yesterday
again

RUNNER

it happens
for my soul
to overtake me
as I run
and my poor body
clenches teeth
to reach it
I run
and while time is immeasurable
my heart is measuring
an hourglass
is crumbling my bones
fast
I run
and my head
like a weirdo
on my shoulders
with a malicious thought
is pecking me
why
and with whom
like a sleepwalker
day in day out
I am racing
as if
I could turn
the hourglass
all by myself

MÖBIUS STRIP

ETERNAL RAIN

You are standing alone among the rain drops
that are hovering around you
like all of my unspoken words
with which I love you
more than the love messages
that flow silently
through all the wires and satellites
and that hold the world
like I hold you in my tender embrace...

I see you through the rain drops,
and each of them -
memory to memory, dream to dream,
life to life is binding
and they are rolling down your face
and you are so beautiful
as much as you were at the beginning, when
outside the time,
you kissed me with the whole time in this world.

Protected by the silence of the rain,
among the drops
and the love like the silhouette of an angel
drawn under the spider web of the rain,
we are standing,
and suddenly you become brightened by the night lightning
in a town that lasted for a second –
yet enough for you to relive
how on the light of your life
with your thoughts like shadows
you are playing on a wall that you don't even know
not even today,
how hard you hit on it with your palms,
when you are waking up with a nightmare on your lips
and that you could never be certain what had really happened
in those constantly changing memories
when I have been dying on your arms...

And it continued,
when a shadow was playing with my body
in that summer night
when the Sun and the Moon and the Sky
were hovering in the rain drops along with the
lightning,
while I was looking at you and while I was
recognizing you,
while you were looking at me
and while you were waiting for me to pronounce
you: My Love...

WITH THE WHOLE TIME I SPEAK TO YOU

There is a time when I grow distant from everything,
when after the deepest sigh
I expect you to show up from nowhere,
and I try
to pull out a moment with only a word,
to ask the moment to pull out an hour for me,
the hour – a day,
the day – a day from tomorrow and the day after
tomorrow
all days – whole time,
and I wonder
will you ever feel the whole time
with which I am talking to you
while you are standing timeless –
with one of your palms blossoming
like the most tender flower
on the cactus of my patience –
and with a handkerchief full of goodbyes
in the other one,
so you could live everywhere with my distances,
some place where our souls
are comforting each other
in their unbreakable balance
and reconciliation in only one word,
with which we become timeless,
a word in which to believe
is the same as to love.

MÖBIUS STRIP

while
as a silent scream
between the sky and the Earth
I am seeking for your navel
on the inner side
you twist
in the thunder flare
that shivers our nudity
and while
from the inside and the outside
we are making love
all of a sudden the Sun
and the Moon
and the sky
meet your eyelash
that from the outer side
of the universe twinkles
with the look
with which I find life
so lovely
so lovely

WHEN THE CLOCK HANDS OVERLAP

with the wagons of the night
I travel
a small
square of light
and
I dream
of a day
when
the Sun
on the circle
of the clock
travels
only for me

and
overlaps with us
my love
at a station when
a sun ray
like a clock hand
in an overlap
with my eye nerve
clicks

CHAIN OF SAND

I was knitting a chain of sand
from the shore to you
and I was waiting
for the sea to pull my chain in

how many rings of moons
I have forged for you
in a chain of tides

one day as endless dream dreamt by the night,
pull out a ring for me
from the chain of the breathing

and when you raise a wave
taller than the wind
and when I am pulled in by the strength
with which you have created the life

be the ring
that I miss for at least a moment, my love
and see how everything begins again...

LITTLE VIGIL LAMP

One day
when the colour of my hair
turns into adornment on someone else's face
and my eyes in someone else's eyes dream
I wonder –
Will they recognize the tremble of love
that like a lonely lantern at the end of the sky
remains lit in the night –
little vigil lamp of the soul
hovering over the shadows of a life...
will I become a better man,
will I know the answers of all departures
when you tell me
that I shouldn't run away from aging,
unless I want to die before my time
and that the lifeline on your palm
is invisible for the eyes, but I will find you anyway,
that I will carry my own years all by myself,
but towards the youth and my childhood they will lead me,
until one beautiful day
through the umbilical cord
of the white wind on the Sun
I see you like a transparent silhouette
that has been walking on foot for a long time
on the longest line of my palm,
and that with the whole time of this world
in just a glance, I will be back between us again...

RED AND WHITE BLOOD CELLS

while
I was juggling
with my red blood cells in a state of panic
you came along
juggling with white blood cells
and while the game of passion was taking place
in which we were mixing all of our cells together
I should be cautious you said to me
at once
because you are not allowed to lose a single cell
you need the white ones to live
and the red ones – to love me

GEOMETRICAL CAT

SHADOW PLAY

all of a sudden
I saw
a shadow
playing
with its own cat
suddenly
the moon
also saw the sun
playing
with my body
in
this town
in which no one knows
why
The Town of Hands
it is called
when
people here
haven't seen their hands
for a long time
and
everything began
with a shadow play
in front of
an
old lamp
with
an imprisoned
spirit

GEOMETRICAL CAT

When the street is sleeping
a geometrical cat
is watching over the traffic in the dream

what we have in common is the light from the past
that comes to us as present time
and, yet the light is walking right now
on the paws of the future

the geometry of night
touches us like a breath on the glass
and the insomnia writes down on them
all the dreams that have never happened before

when the street is sleeping
a black cat passes by like a gigantic shadow
over the graphite
that says that only the awakened ones
don't dream like automats

THE BALD TOWN

One beautiful day
being chased by the thoughts
     the hat was running
running
     and the wind
at the corner
     took it
swirled it up to the skyscraper at once
and asked it
     - Where are you coming from?
     Where are you running to?!
- Put me on your head
     and you'll know,
you'll know everything about the bald town
- Come on, come on
let him run after me
let him think that I am kidnapped,
demand a ransom
for his metropolitan ideas,
for his phantasms
that after the Orson Welles,
     the asteroids
aligned by the Pythagorean theorem
will be hitting the towns again
     with massive hysterias
- Oh, please – blew the wind
- Hey you, wanderer, you don't believe me, huh?
- Well, who would want to live
in a bald town
in which no flea
has its privacy,
     yet everyone knows –
every real town
was born and raised under a hat
with enough illusions over the brim
and
occasional escapes
     from its-own thoughts
and

I am such a hat exactly!
Am I not, brother –
             the hat
convinced the wind
             and they went away together
far a way from the town
             far, far a way
from the thoughts...

THE QUEEN OF THE TRANSPARENT CHESS PIECES

with my double who doesn't think like a double,
I am playing chess –
he, with his black chess pieces, and I – with my
transparent thoughts. When between the East and
the West he moves, he sunsets in one of my
thoughts that knows - he was me long time ago;
when I sunrise with all shadows
like pawns in front of me,
he takes them and from my back
he attacks me with the Trojan horse of the night.
In the game, he is my enemy,
and he is constantly attacking me with me,
because he knows that in the real life
my real enemy is me myself,
although I am not aware that he is me,
and the only predictability
with which I could beat him
is that he thinks that he is me,
and when he is going after me,
I know how the bishop in me thinks
Nevertheless, I have a weakness –
I have never felt like a king, although I have always
wanted the queen
of all my transparent chess pieces...

WHAT DID CHARLIE CH. SEE FROM THE UPSIDE DOWN

Here comes Charlie Ch. winded up as a toy
- You, idiot/ he whispers to me/
and he turns himself upside down all of a sudden
and he hooks himself with his long feet on the tightrope,
he lets my blood flow unstoppably on the wire of a nerve fibre
he sharply lifts the tails of his little tailcoat
one by one
with the kicks of his heels
he becomes a dot among the dots...
What did Charlie Ch. see from the upside down?
We were eating fish – he was carefully sucking the bones of the shoe
/I – the tacks of the sheatfish/
we were throwing the leftovers to the garbage cans
which were hopping from the orgasm-m-m-m-m-m
of the cats
- Hurry up, Charlie, hurry up
A volcano that turns into typhoon
(you don't see it) your foot is stuck on the floor with a chewing gum,
and it is already clear that it is a giant from the waist to the head
and he is shooting at us, oh, he is shooting at us from the distance!
- Hurry up, Charlie, detach yourself! Free yourself!
What?
You are in love. Such a mess! You are in love
Charlie
/the head of your soul is out of the skull/
A black rock, a sad one
is hovering in my head, right now, Charlie
The typewriter is beating out of my heart,
and the sheet is hopelessly white, although electricity went off...
Although electricity is gone, I know that deep down

in the white
I feel
My blood is close/ to the other side/ And it is time
for me to wake up,
although I don't know where...
You... You have been laughing from the upside
down, haven't you, Charlie?

BLACK-AND-WHITE RUSHING TOWN

With the left and the right epilepsy
                                                of the eyelashes
all in love
on your knees, you fall, Charlie,
                                                swiftly, swiftly
you come loose
with the left and the right fly
                                                quickly, quickly
/or with a faintheartedness too fast/
                                                you juggle
with the cheekbones in the black-and-white rushing
town
------ all of a sudden
                        Caught
                                Rolled over by the great
Mechanism /levers, gearwheels, springs
                                                and so on/
you salute from the full-blooded Führer

with toothbrush moustache /identically overlapped/
with a balloon in which the world is inflated
you juggle, you salute, you juggle /stand straight
and tuck your stomach in!/ juggle Charlie
while the gravitation is hovering
and the laughter is blowing us
and until the world bursts again - - - - - and I /what I?!/
where am I /?/
        -        Well, here you are, here – between the right
                                        And the left fly Charlie

A ROOM ENVELOPE

I take
my double out of my head
carefully
and I fold the room into an envelope
I address the letter
to a distant country
and
I say
If someone
reads this sad letter
aloud
he or she should be careful
because it could push
this room down the stairs
when he or she like a totally different person
at the end of the world
opens
that long expected letter
with words that
dissolve
from the paper
leaving
white human mountains behind

SYMMETRICAL DOUBLE

please
chase
away
the flies
from the mirror
we smell
like death
more than before
my
symmetrical
double

asked me
silently
and I
thought
feverishly
why
it
wasn't
me
who raised
that question
at the first place

HORIZON OF LIVING

HORIZON OF LIVING

No, I am not happy with you
you live before your time
no, there is no room for me there
my body tells me

you are wrong, you are wrong
nothing exists
if time and space are apart
if you and I are apart
from the horizon of our living

I say that to my body
that takes up space in the future
not being aware that
that is the only way the future can be created

I am not, I am not happy with you
it is so tight in here and I can hardly breathe
I feel like I am an embryo
should I give you a birth one more time

my body tells me, and I beg it
to bear just a moment only
after that we will not be just a cultural layer
under the horizon of living

OTHER-SIDED HORSE

My this-sided Trojan horse
has nothing to do with the other-sided war
for Helen of Troy,
neither with despair, nor with the ship's ribs of the storms
out of which it is forged.

For the this-sided Trojan horse
I am the other-sided Laocoon
who throws the spear towards him-self constantly
and this-sided "I"
doesn't even blink in the heart of the horse.

My this-sided horse
doesn't forget to let the two sea serpents go
and to strangle me with my other-sided sons.

My other-sided horse
is in a tragic union with Priam, the King,
when all of us - this-sided men
accept the gift of the Gods.

Yet, while many people
are waiting for my notorious end,
as their greatest desire, could you, please,
imagine for a moment, My king,
what kind of this-sided man you are
if you have other-sided thoughts?

BEAT

with red blood cells
juggling often
from my fingers
swarms of people
come out and run
and they
and I
we are all passionately perfecting,
they – in the ability
to keep the blood
from falling
on the paper, and
I - in the ability to strengthen
the heart beat
to the colossal muteness
in the middle of the bloodthirsty audience
where she sits as well,
my darling,
furiously angry
and fully aware
of my compulsive vice
to play
with
myself
inside

FOG 1

I had chosen
a street in the fog
convinced
that I am on the right address
I lifted
the letter from the threshold
and I left
the door open
through which
my
mad house
escaped from me again

FOG 2

I had chosen
a street for me in the fog
that took me to the town
I lifted the letter on the threshold
I let the windup toy
pass through the door
and I
I had firm conviction
that it was the right address

LITTLE COLLAR DOVE

Each spring on the window lands
and with its black crescent around the nape
adorns itself and looks at its own reflection,
the collar dove with its wedding apron

and with the beak of gold from the golden pollen
of the pine trees
it adorns the mirror
but the truth is – it adorns me and it nudges me
from the other side of the glass
to make me postpone cutting off the old pine tree
with a nest in it, like every year before

DOUBLE

Far away from home, in the waiting room of a railway station,
all of a sudden, I was captivated by a young woman's gaze.
She approached to me as she was enchanted and said
that I look like her brother, which was horribly unbelievable.
And she started telling me about him in details,
he had gone to war,
got married, and her niece was born,
and she has got our eyes,
he had been in a fierce quarrel with his father for his persistence to go to war.

Suddenly, she went through the scar over my arcade
with her forefinger telling me that he, her brother, didn't have one –
how did you get this, she asked me,
A snowball with a rock inside got me when I was a kid – I said.
There were lots of questions in her eyes,
but she couldn't ask me for my name either
because there was no time –
oh! do you remember that our roof was full of doves,
and you were telling me that we were living under the umbrella of love cooing
- she was cooing to me, and I looked at the stone prayer for the bliss of the saints and the apostilles over the near cathedral
and I had to get into the train responding for the last passenger call.
I went far away with my muted answers –
I was going to war, as well
to the other side of the border – against myself alone!

MICHELANGELO AND MY FATHER'S HEART

MICHELANGELO AND MY FATHER'S HEART

The will of the Almighty, Michelangelo has painted
as a red shroud in a shape of uncovered brain,
by touching Adam with the forefinger of immortality,
to tell us that all the knots on the sky
are tangled in our heads,
and sometimes a knot untangles
and like an umbilical cord
goes down
to conceive the silent embryo of the word in us ...
I was thinking about this while I was sitting next to
my father in the fast ambulance car and next to his
weak heart with the pacemaker's impulses
and the electrodes pierced in his heart muscle.
I was thinking, as well, about the harp traveling
in the very same laying position like my father
with wires vibrant on the bumpy road.
And I was having these thoughts, while I was
holding his hand and his pulse
with which he was coming back to our lives on the
bumpy road...

GLIMPSE

the time is a pupil
that expands and contracts
with the spirits
of the dead and the unborn
and all of a sudden
you see
that the light
with the gloom, too,
gives you a glimpse

BIRTHDAY GREETING

On the other side of the world, it's my birthday
already
although I wasn't born
in the time of my birth yet,
from the other side of the world
a birthday greeting, I received.

How wonderful it is to know
that on a distant meridian
the time of our birth
will never be touched
by the time of our death

THE NIGHT FACE OF THE SUN

The apples were ripening with the morning light,
and the palm was ripening around the apple as well,
the apples were also ripening quietly with the full moon
that was showing us the face of the Sun in the gloom

A lightning broke into the old house
like a heated apple, and grandpa opened the windows
to avoid the lightning to hit the walls of the poor little
rooms and spoke
a free soul shouldn't be stopped

The carps were jumping out of the calm water
splashing the moon in circles of vocals
A human landed on the Moon for the first time
and bounced free from the gravity
and the weight of the mind

I and my friend from my childhood, Elijah
were lying back and thinking loudly with the bright stars
looking at the infinite diamond of cosmos
grinded in innumerable angles that flashed with the
whole time

We started to crave to keep our time safe
in one flight even before we spread our wings,
not knowing that we were a threat to ourselves
and the life and the death wanted more than each other

Our palms became ripe around the apple
and the apples were ripening quietly with the full moon,
then you showed us peacefully, dear God,
the night face of the Sun
as a fruit that can't be picked
by the silence of the perfection

SIMULTANEOUS TIME

the puppy was pressing the piano keys
with its front legs
and with its nose and paws afterwards
looking for the sounds under the synthesizer

I am looking for the time that I don't have
just like that puppy

the puppy and I sometimes feel
that the time is simultaneous
it is almost impossible, at the same time,
to have all
that makes you happy

EIGHT MINUTES OF DAY IN THE NIGHT

As I was coming back home in the late hours
a bundle of light pressed my shadow
against my front door.

The shadow opened the door
and entered inside the house
in the very same moment
as the light went off,
and I was left outside the house.

No, this wasn't a dream,
because my dream has been complaining to me for
so long
that my house is constantly open
for all spectres that tear themselves apart of the
night, that it becomes more and more difficult
to wake me up
simultaneously with the light
being late for only eight minutes
until I recall that
my day is also late in the lateness –
eight minutes
after the night has come
just to be on time
everywhere where I must or I mustn't be

THE WHITE MOUSE OF THE TRUTH

When I was a little boy,
and my mother was taking me to the bazaar,
by the old house at the end of the cobblestone street,
a blind man was standing
with a wooden box with two compartments in his hands.

There was a white mouse in one,
and leaves of fortunes – in the other.
My mother was buying goods starting from there
and from that fortune teller
she was purchasing our fortunes.

The mouse would start sniffing our life line on our palms,
and then it would bite the leaf.
Speaking of the fortune, illiterate as I was,
my mother used to read it to me aloud,
although she kept silent sometimes, and I couldn't tell
why.

And I learned to read, early,
so I could read my fortune all by myself
even when it was not supposed to be read or told,
and when I became literate, I realized, in time,
that each word is a compartment of a labyrinth
from which you can get out only if you can read aloud
to someone
from whom you would rather hide
the white mouse of the truth.

SCULPTURE OF BREATHING

VERB (in)TENSE(ness)

the devil speaks with tensed vowels as he is becoming
present tense in the tenseness of time,
while he is melting the iceberg of the adjectives attached
to the nouns
and wipes the time's face of the verb tense from the
sense

and all began near the people of the paradise that were
sitting at the table
when he was sent down
from the abstract chain ring of the hell
to make the first crime in the language

and so,
the juices that those happy people were drinking,
he decided to cook with the fire of his own verbs –
he turned the fire into a vapor,
and the vapor into the liquid thread

everyone came to the pipe of the condenser asking him:
What are you doing, you handsome boy, and he said –
paradise water so you can be joyfully delighted and
happily happy

and the paradise people, oh the dearest ones, they
approached and started to drink
and they felt so excited – ecstatically euphoric
and all fruits were blooming becoming ripe in their songs

all of this was observed by his fathers all in flame
and they couldn't believe their eyes – what a peevish
fool their son was to do good for the people
so they started to judge that adorned rogue, until

oh, until the first evil word came out to peck and sting
and until the heart of the adjective got stabbed
by the first knife
that is how and why, since Cain and Abel, we are
turning each other into ashes

THRESHING TIME

the time has changed
in our old house yard
the pole was left all alone
untouched by the changes
the Sun is spinning its shadow only
with the white grandpa's horses

once upon a time the bread was being threshed
today we need the wheat of time
to make time before the apocalypse happens

and like a wooden pole
I am standing in the middle of the word's yard
and with the white grandpa's horses
I am threshing time for my children

CAT TIMES

We have been raised by altar bread.
Our childhood was grapevines for us
on which the young wine was ripening on our sky.

We grew up in a time
when we could buy fresh chickpea bread
or we could visit the ivied summer cinema at night

We watched Tornatore's movies
and we were kids with the kids from the movie.

We didn't know what fascism is,
we thought communism will last forever,
and we loved to play mobsters.

Our most favourite scene of all
was when we were staffing the fat Ollie's mouth
with hunks of white socialist bread,
and he wasn't complaining about it, because he
was always hungry.

On the summer provincial movie screen,
America was Marilyn Monroe for us –
Marilyn Monroe rising up into the Statue of Liberty.

Under the wind of her little dress,
she was revealing to us the colonization,
Mad Horse, Sitting Bull as he is acting himself
and swearing in the circus that rises up to her
panties
in which there is no place
for the children of Cheyenne raised by their
mothers
so they could be killed as little shooting targets in
the air.

There wasn't a place for the civil war, too,
nor for the prohibition, and

the gangsters with automats,
but there was a place for Chaplin's toothbrush
moustaches
and his two fingers with which
he blocks his ears
to prevent the lion from awakening,
for Buster Keaton's frozen face
and the house that spins the storm,
and he can't get through the door in any way,
and for Orson Welles' Martians
with which he performed radio invasion
with the same fear as the fear of Cold War.

There is no place in Monroe's panties
for the helicopters' Flight of the Bumblebee in the
apocalypse of napalm,
nor for the underground hangars with
intercontinental rockets,
but there is a place for the Jedis from Star Wars
that hold the torch of liberty with their thoughts
in the middle of the darkness of the universe.

We have been raised by altar bread,
we have become democrats, too,
and we have spent nine cat lives
so we could survive,
but no one wants to remember the death between
them.

I was left only with the memories
when my grandfather Carlo, the emigrant,
returned from America with a black limousine
and a blond girl,
Marilyn Monroe he said she was,
and we were just kids,
so we believed him without any questioning,
because we recognized her for her panties
when we stumbled on purpose and fell under her
little dress.

SCULPTURE OF BREATHING

the potter put a ball of alabaster
                                                                          on the wheel
- throat lump of what has yet to be expressed
and on the wheel
                                            of the breathing – me.

The potter threw and twisted the white clay –
with one hand inside
and with the other hand outside –
And with my breath outside
                                                      and my sigh
inside, I was throwing and twisting and removing
syllables
for nothing to be in excess
when the air starts to tremble between us.

And when the shadow
                                                     of the white vase
revealed the light line
in the little shop
like a swallow nest
covered with birdy bites of clay
I remained silent
in the middle of the sculpture of breathing
and for a long time,
I was reading from the beauty lips
for nothing to be in excess
                                                            when
the white flower petals of spring alight on our palms
and the invisible bond of the words
eventually makes us believe
that everything is as it should be...

FOSSIL HESITATION

the morning touched me with the forefinger of a day
the day – with a moment
the moment with the whole time
and I was running
being pushed by the forefinger in front of the whole time
and my body
was the only space and time
like a large ship full of words
nevertheless
the flood of the unspoken words
cannot explain the fossils of the days,
fossils in which I failed to speak out all the injustice
and I know – on a square meter of the Earth
up to the edge of the universe we are being
pressed by 10 N
or 1 kg of air
and the morning pressed me with the forefinger of a day
the day – with a moment
the moment with the whole time
the whole time with the question
How much does an unspoken word
hesitate between the life and the chaos weigh?

THE POET'S ANGEL

My angel
says
that
he himself
is
an
angel
fallen
as
an anchor
at the bottom
of
God's
glory

ARS POETICA

the room that I am meditating in
touches me with its forefinger –
pointing towards my head,
but it aims at my thoughts,
and there she goes out of the house,
while I am out of reach
of the speed and the impulse of the sleeplessness
and yet, there is a sweat between the volume
and the temperature of the thoughts
from which it is impossible to escape
but it quite possible to ignite and to burn
into fine white ashes
invisible on the white paper
the true wisdom is
to know how to hold your breath
and how to let it out at the right moment –
to blow out the ashes
and to show what has been written

POETRY

this mirror
is the smoothest
shaved cheek
on which
the beard
of time
stopped growing
so
be careful
you could easily
become sad
when
you stand
in front of it

ORIGAMI

I folded the paper
Into white birds,
and from the highest building in the town
I let them fly
and then I ran down the stairs
to catch them landing in my hands –
just like I used to do as a child.

When I got down
the birds were circling over the square.
I stood and waited
for each of them to land.
I was waiting and hoping
that someone will read
those few words
that I had written on their wings.

Suddenly, in a breathtaking moment,
my words
like birds
started to dance on the sky again.

DIPTYCH OF THE SORROW

1.
The ancient Chinese physicians
thought of sorrow as a lung disease

I often wonder
how little oxygen is there in the sorrow
and how is it possible a sky of the word to be
created
from such a little amount of oxygen.

It is amazing how we are interweaving like two
flames
that burn out of the same root – my hand was
speaking to me and was writing down all that I
didn't want to tell her about the joy.

2. Poet,
have you heard that the ancient Chinese physicians
thought of sorrow as a lung disease,
have you ever wondered
how little oxygen is there in the sorrow?

It is amazing how the sky of the word is created
from such a little amount of oxygen,
it is amazing how we are interweaving like two
flames
that burn out of the same root –
my hand was speaking to me and was writing down
all that I didn't want to tell her about the joy.

HOUSE SPIDER WEB

Have you ever thought
that the spider web spread in the house
is the most tender organ of your house,
that everything you mutter with the nightmare's lips
it absorbs with the softness of the room's angles
and because of it
the angles can't be seen as a geometry of
finiteness anymore
a geometry that spins your silence as well,
and the little spider that lives in it
hunts your breathing from the ambush
with the sighs crucified among the walls.

Have you ever asked yourselves in the times
when all the rocks are falling apart from it
and are hovering around you like dreams
why it becomes a swallow
that unstoppably flies in the house
to remember all of the air entrances
to the nest of saliva and mud under the threshold.

Have you ever asked yourselves
why when the autumn shortens the day
a strange wind like a warm path of air
raises your hands disembodiedly
before a long migration
with which the day starts to grow again
as lungs of a chained night…

READING FROM RIGHT TO LEFT

If your windows are misty and moisty in the morning
–
they are wet because of the breathing of your dreams
meaning that the room in which you sleep
is a womb that protects you from the cold.
If it is too cold,
the dreams will be frozen like a frost flower
in the floral garden of the winter that has already stepped in.
On the glade of the awakening,
no one can ever see what you have been dreaming,
unless you write something on the window glass.
That is how poets write down their dreams –
and you have to learn to read from right to left.
And it turns out to be good,
because that writing which has the end of the thought
as the beginning of the feeling
never ends...

BENEVOLENCE HANGER

BENEVOLENCE HANGER

it stands like a stripped Christmas tree
with two buns instead of baubles
among the snowflakes
and says:
If you have something to give, hang it,
if you don't have, take what is left

a good man has put it on the street
and I was wondering what should we hang
as an offer for the children of the future

If you have something to give, hang it,
if you don't have, take what is left
I was telling myself while I was hanging
all of my unspoken words one by one

I was arranging the silence snowflake by snowflake
and the breathing sigh by sigh
the breathing with which God was creating us
breath by breath

LISTEN ROOSTER*

listen verdant
                listen high
                              Stream listen Serpent
listen Scops Owl and Night
          listen Rooster at Midnight
listen water
                arched into a Bow
                          listen Arrow
and a Lake, listen rooster, listen rooster
Vortex of Shadows
                listen Ash tree blue
listen Rain, listen rain, rain and fume
listen easiness
        listen blue
                trembling white
listen Doe
      from a Spring
               listen screech in the Eye
among the beech trees
              dark listen leafy rustle
listen Scops Owl and Night
          listen Rooster at Midnight
A Mushroom
        listen Worm in gentle growth
listen Falcon
            hot listen
            Heart
aimed by Thunder, through the branches
listen jingle
        Wind and fulgurating echo
in the Pupil engraved
                glare listen distant
under the palate
            listen Breath
                    iron listen
bite into blood, listen bite into Blood
made by wolf's yearn
                listen gust, listen gust

listen Scops Owl and Night
        listen Snow at Midnight

---
*name of a mountain peak in North Macedonia

THE ARTIST OF DEATH

He has been making up death for his whole life
he has been filing her nails,
shaving her beard,
trimming her moustaches,
putting mascara on her eyelashes,
cutting her hair, making pedicure, nail polishing,
and
applying liquid and powder foundation,
he has been making her up with a smile – a
discrete one
like Mona Lisa's smile,
he was doing her makeover like a nice memory,
just for a moment –
to be beautiful before the earth covers her
appearance,
before she becomes bodiless – a memory only!

"In my dreams, the dead are coming to me,
they are angry with me
because I have forgotten their golden watches,
or because I have tied their shoes with one knot
only,
she wanted white instead of a yellow rose
yellow reminds us of the betrayal,
she is angry because I have drawn grimace too
severe and cold,
in spite of the fact that she was righteous judge,
and she wasn't as much as pretty when she was
alive
as she is now as a dead woman,
and now as a result all people will have memories
of her prettier death,
that she has never wanted me to cover her wrinkles
under her eyes
with which she was happy,
that she has never worn a bow tie,
nor a shirt with little snob wings –
death is miserable among the rich,
she is neither a man nor a woman", he would say.

When my father passed away,
we put cardboard shoes on his feet,
and he didn't complain –andwe were grieving over
his death.
And that is how my life was,
and I am thinking to outwit her with me –
I will turn myself into ash,
and the wind will be my grave,
and when the wind starts to blow from the East,
someone will remember that I was a shepherd
before I went to America,
and will drink hot Rakia in my name...

THE MORNING LINE

Every morning a man with a little white dog
goes out in the street
shaded by the graphite pencil of the dream

the belt of the awakening pulls the man
and the night unties the dippers of the light
until the baby of the day starts cooing

the soft morning light started to snow
on the branches over the roofs and on the horizon
and she is walking with a light step over the
footprints and the paws.

a man and his little dog in the distance
become a white dot and an echo that comes back
to the pencil whence the morning line untangles

BREAD

take a flour and a soul
to be a yeast of the body
and mix it

the dough is so soft at the beginning
and tender on touch
almost like a liquid
Lightly flour a cotton cloth
and roll the dough out as much as you can
by folding it on each side
tender and soft like a placenta
it fills up with air bubbles
and becomes fluffy

full with the souls of the living and the dead
connected with the air bubbles under the crust
the bread is baking
and time comes when she takes the bread to her
father's house
and to her sister's house
and to her brother's house

no, it wasn't bread for the soul that people give to
each other
in the memory of the people who are not with them
anymore
The bread connects us as the spikelet connects the
grains
she used to say and with a tear she was hydrating
the bread
that was entering her home with some of her
loved ones

EVERLASTING MOMENT

The artist painted the angel like a sunrise
the angel lifted up his wings spread them widely and
said to him:
*Good morning
the moments are more precious than the eternity*

The mother looked at the toys
hung on the clothes line
and one of the dolls with a mechanism
irritated by the water cried after her persistently:
Ma-ma, ma-ma,...

because the moments are more precious
than the eternity

The old man raised the glass of wine
and made a toast in honour of death,
because death was still waiting for him,
yet she hated herself
for having to wait for someone all the time

and the moments are more precious than the eternity

We are wading through labyrinths constantly –
the traveler thought and
aimless traveling is the best – he said,
because we don't have to stop
even when the previous labyrinth is a dead-end
in the next one

because the moments are more precious
than the eternity

The artist painted the angel like a sunset
and he lifted up the wings and spread them widely again
and rose up on the other side of the Earth

because the moments are more precious
than the eternity

GILGAMESH

when
with a third of a man
transparent fiber roots
towards the sky I was sprouting
when with bitter fruits
the wisdom of the Earth
with two thirds of love
I was tasting
I lost my mind over an unhappy love
Oh, Gilgamesh, my brother
even today
I cannot escape your fate
- one third of a man
and two thirds of a yearn
I am
constantly

ABOUT THE AUTHOR

BORCHE PANOV
Republic of North Macedonia

Borche Panov was born on September 27, 1961 in Radovish, Republic of North Macedonia. He graduated from the "Sts. Cyril and Methodius" University of Skopje, Faculty of Filology in the filed of Macedonian and South Slavic Languages in 1986. Panov has been a member of the Macedonian Writers' Association since 1998. He published 15 poetry books and 8 plays in Macedonian language. He has also published poetry books in other languages: "Hematite particles" (2016 - in Macedonian and Bulgarian and "Photostiheza" 2019, Bulgaria), "Vdah" in Slovenian (2017, Slovenia), "Shaving balloon" in Serbian (2018, Serbia), "Blood that juggles 8000 poetic thoughts" in Croatian (2021, Croatia), "Underground Apple" in Arabic language (United Arab Emirates, 2021), "Underground apple" in English (Netherlands, 2021), "Dandelion Cadence" in English (co-author, India, 2021), "Sculpture of Breathing" in Italian and English (2022, Italy), "The Morning Line" in Romanian (2023, Romania). His poetry has been translated into 40 languages and published all around the world. He received many literary awards such as the following: Premio Mondiale "Tulliola-Renato Filippelli" in Italy for his book "Shaving the Balloon" (2021), "City of Galateo-Antonio De Ferraris" (Italy, Rome, 2021), Premio "Le Occasioni" in Italy, the Sahito World Literary Award in 2021, Predrag Matvejevic in Croatia for his book "Shaving Balloon", Naji Niman Award in 2022. He has edited many poetry books and poetry anthologies and has launched many authors and books published in Macedonia. He also translates poetry from Macedonian into Serbian and Croatian language and vice versa. Panov works as a Counselor for Culture and Education at the Municipality of Radovish, and he is also a president of the program board of the "International Karamanov's Poetry Festival" for more than 20 years.

ABOUT THE TRANSLATOR

Daniela Andonovska-Trajkovska (1979, Bitola, Republic of North Macedonia) is a poetess, author, scientist, editor in chief of two literary magazines in North Macedonia, literary critic, doctor of pedagogy, university professor at the University "Kliment Ohridski" Bitola (Faculty of Education), a member of the Macedonian Writers' Association; Macedonian Science Society – Bitola; Slavic Academy for Literature and Art in Varna – Bulgaria, and Bitola Literary Circle. She was president of the Macedonian Science Society Editorial Council and now – a head of the Linguistics and Literature Department at the Macedonian Science Society – Bitola. She has published two books of stories, 9 poetry books, one book for children, a book of literary criticism in Macedonian and 3 academic and scientific books that are part of the curriculum at the university where she works, and over 100 scientific articles. She has also 6 poetry books published in English, Italian, Arabic and Romanian language in India, United Arab Emirates, Italy, and Romania. She has also published her translations from English into Macedonian and vice versa in North Macedonia, Italy and Netherland (7 poetry books and many articles). She has won several important awards for literature: "Krste Chachanski (2018); "Karamanov" for "Electronic Blood" (2019); Macedonian Literary Avant-garde for "House of Contrasts" (2020); "Abduvali Qutbiddin" (2020, Uzbekistan); Premio Mondiale "Tulliola- Renato Filippelli" in Italy for "Electronic Blood" (2021); Award of excellence "City of Galateo - Antonio De Ferrariis" (Italy); Award for Literary Criticism in 2022, Poetry Award "Dritero Agioli" (Albania, 2023); Poetry Award "Mihai Eminescu", a Golden Medal and a recognition as ambassador of culture in Romania by the Mihai Eminescu Academy (2023) and "Aco Shopov" for poetry (the most important national poetry prize by Macedonian Writers' Association in 2021). Her poetry has been translated and published into more than 40 world languages.

www.ingramcontent.com/pod-product-compliance
Lightning Source LLC
Chambersburg PA
CBHW020358170426
43200CB00005B/219